Y0-EKT-049

AN OLD FASHIONED

Norman Rockwell Christmas

Hal Leonard Publishing Corporation
7777 West Bluemound Road
P.O. Box 13819 Milwaukee, Wisconsin 53213

Published by HAL LEONARD PUBLISHING CORPORATION
P.O. Box 13819, 7777 West Bluemound Road
Milwaukee, WI 53213 USA

Contents

© Hallmark Cards, Inc.

The Sounds of Christmas

Music is an important feature of Norman Rockwell's art. This may sound like an unusual claim to make about an illustrator but it is, nevertheless, true. The characters that Rockwell painted for Hallmark are all having fun celebrating the Christmas season and this means that music *must* be part of the picture.

When you look at the illustrations in this book you will surely hear the sounds of Christmas running through your head. Rockwell's characters seem to dance and sing even though their images are locked for all time in the pose that he chose for them. How easy it is to imagine that the cellist is playing "Deck The Halls" as the little girl and her dog dance, or that the well-scrubbed choirboy is singing "Joy To The World" with all his heart while the cherubs provide an accompaniment.

Because music was such an important aspect of Rockwell's life and work, it is fitting that, at long last, his illustrations are themselves being surrounded by music. The familiar carols in this collection are the very ones that Rockwell grew up with and that he sang as a choirboy. They are the Christmas songs that he enjoyed sharing with his family and friends throughout his life.

We hope that *An Old Fashioned Norman Rockwell Christmas* will be a Christmas present that you will share with your family and friends for many years to come.

GOOD BOYS & GIRLS
Norman Rockwell

A Picture-Perfect Christmas

by Patrick Byrne

Glistening, gently falling snow…harmonious, caroling voices…jingling sleigh bells…the sweet scent of freshly-cut pine trees…tasty eggnog…a palette of sugar cookies…children nervously awaiting a visit from a kindly Santa Claus…These are some of the ingredients for a picture-perfect Christmas; the kind of Christmas that all of us dream about. These dreams of a white Christmas probably look very much like the illustrations of Norman Rockwell. More than any other artist of his day — and it was a very long day, spanning six decades — Rockwell succeeded in depicting the Christmas dreams of several generations of Americans.

When Norman Rockwell accepted a commission from Hallmark Cards in 1948, he was already firmly established as the greatest American illustrator of the century. Rockwell was personally asked by Hallmark founder J.C. Hall to illustrate — what else? — Christmas cards. Rockwell would eventually create about three dozen cards for Hallmark. Twenty eight of these wonderful illustrations grace the pages of this book.

© Hallmark Cards, Inc.

These Hallmark cards represent Rockwell at his very best. All of the images have a warm-hearted, nostalgic feel that was always such an endearing element of his style. Another quality that is easy to spot in these illustrations is Rockwell's sense of humor. Sometimes the joke is obvious: a man precariously perched on a ladder trying to place a star on the top of a sad, spindly Christmas tree while his patient wife steadies him by holding his belt. Meanwhile, two yapping canines chase a black cat around the base of the ladder. It's the kind of comic scene that can't help but make you smile as you imagine what might happen next.

A more subtle wit can be found in Rockwell's portrait of a choirboy surrounded by musical cherubs. As a child Rockwell had

Norman
Rockwell

spent many hours as a choirboy at St. Luke's and the Cathedral of St. John The Divine in New York City. His choir schedule would sometimes include singing four services on a Sunday plus attending four rehearsals during the week. Needless to say, Rockwell made good use of this personal experience every time he was called on to paint an enthusiastic choirboy trying his best to sound and look like an angel.

Santa Claus is the main character in almost half of the cards that Rockwell designed for Hallmark. He always differentiates between the real, often haloed, St. Nick and the vain attempts by people to fill the great man's trousers. The real Santa appears much as we would expect him to from the description of him given in Clement Moore's "'Twas The Night Before Christmas:" a kindly, jolly old elf whose round tummy looks as if it probably would shake like a bowl of jelly. The only time that Rockwell goes beyond this classic portrait is when he portrays St. Nick as he surely must be on the morning after his annual trek around the world: bug-eyed, stressed out, and exhausted. This is an image of the real Santa to which many parents can relate.

Whenever people try to dress up like Santa Claus there is bound to be some laughs. Whether it is an odd-couple team of Salvation Army Santas or a screaming brat yanking on a fake beard, Rockwell knows how to make these good-natured scenes work. He can also make us chuckle when a little boy spies Santa kissing Mommy or, borrowing a trick from the Dutch masters, we see ourselves in a mirror at the instant that — a few minutes too soon — we discover Santa's secret.

But it isn't just Santa Claus who bears gifts at Christmas. Santa's generous spirit can also appear in the guise of a friendly letter carrier laden with presents or a young woman on the last leg of her journey home for the holidays. Norman Rockwell's personal gift to all of us at Christmas is found in these wonderful Hallmark illustrations that seem to make real the Christmas images that we have all dreamt about.

Norman
Rockwell

Norman Rockwell

Although most of Norman Rockwell's illustrations depict life in small town, rural America, he was actually a city boy born on February 3, 1894, in New York City on the Upper West Side of Manhattan at 103rd Street and Amsterdam Avenue. Rockwell's father was the manager of the New York office of George Woods, Sons, Company, a textile firm. The Rockwells were comfortably affluent and, in 1903, they were able to move from Manhattan to the more tranquil, suburban environment of Mamaroneck.

After business hours Rockwell's father pursued the creative hobby of copying illustrations from magazines. A fine role model for his son, but the more probable source of Rockwell's innate artistic gifts was his maternal grandfather, Thomas Hill, who immigrated to the United States from England shortly after the Civil War. Hill was a painter by trade. He specialized in finely detailed and highly realistic illustrations of animals. These scenes profoundly impressed his grandson. Writing in his autobiography many years later Rockwell still remembered that Hill: "painted in great detail — every hair on the dog was carefully drawn; the tiny highlights in the pig's eyes — great, watery human eyes — could clearly be seen." These were exactly the type of stylistic characteristics that Rockwell inherited from Hill and gladly retained in his own works.

Rockwell was a born artist and by the time he was an adolescent he knew that painting was the career that he wanted to pursue. He dropped out of high school during his sophomore year in order to devote himself completely to studying art. His prodigious talents needed very little in the way of formal training and his professional career began in 1910 when he was only sixteen years old. His first commission was to design four Christmas Cards. A year later his first illustrated book, *Tell Me Why Stories*, was published. He was hired the following year — for the princely salary of fifty dollars a month — to be the Art Director of *Boy's Life*, the new official magazine of the fledgling Boy Scouts of America. It was during Rockwell's years at *Boys Life* that he developed his uncanny knack for painting cover illustrations.

© Hallmark Cards, Inc.

In 1916, while still employed by *Boys Life*, an older artist convinced Rockwell that he should submit some of his cover ideas to what had long been America's preeminent weekly magazine: the prestigious *Saturday Evening Post*. Buoyed by his friend's moral support and kindly encouragement, Rockwell carefully finished two cover paintings and prepared a sketch of a third idea. He then set off to visit the *Post's* editorial offices in Philadelphia.

The gangly twenty-one year old artist — he was almost six feet tall but barely weighed 135 pounds — arrived at this pinnacle of the publishing world unheralded and unannounced. While the *Post's* Art Director examined his meager portfolio in a private office, Rockwell was left to sit nervously in the waiting room. When the Art Director finally emerged from the *Post's* inner sanctum with his verdict he excitedly announced that he wanted to use both of Rockwell's paintings for cover illustrations. He also urged Rockwell to complete the sketched idea as quickly as possible so that it could be purchased as well. He then informed the flabbergasted young artist that the *Post* wanted to order three more of his paintings!

Rockwell's first *Saturday Evening Post* cover appeared on May 20, 1916. Over the next 47 years his fame and fortune grew by leaps and bounds as the number of his *Post* covers and illustrations steadily increased, eventually totaling in the hundreds. His last *Post* cover appeared in 1963.

After fifty years of intense creative work, and at a time in life when most people are happy to retire and take it easy, Rockwell left the *Post* to find a new challenge. The result was the series of memorable covers and illustrations that he painted for *Look* magazine. Contributing to a major news magazine for the first time in his life, Rockwell was no longer asked to paint the American Dream but to witness the American reality of the turbulent sixties: the Peace Corps, the Civil Rights movement, and, in 1969 — at the age of seventy five — the Apollo 11 Space Team.

When Norman Rockwell died in 1978, he was the most well-known and best-loved American painter of the century. He had created a tremendously popular style of art that was instantly identifiable as being his own distinct brand of Americana. Along with Woody Guthrie's songs of the dust bowl, and Frank Capra's great films of the 1930s and 1940s — including the Christmas classic: *It's A Wonderful Life* (1946) — Rockwell's illustrations ennobled the traditional American family as the bedrock of democracy. His reassuring images of rural nostalgia and traditional values counteracted the turbulent waves of modernism that buffeted the world throughout the twentieth century. Today, one hundred years after Rockwell's birth, his illustrations remain a comforting vision of the strength of the average American.

Norman Rockwell and Hallmark Cards

illustration:
"The Kansas City Spirit"

Norman Rockwell had already been associated with Hallmark Cards for several years when tragedy struck the company's headquarters in Kansas City. On Friday, July 13, 1951, the Missouri River became a raging torrent and the Hallmark warehouses, situated near the banks of the river, were devastated by over six feet of flood water. Beyond the tremendous material loss for Hallmark, the flood ravaged a large part of the city, destroying the stockyards and severely damaging the railway lines that served the city.

When news of this catastrophe reached Norman Rockwell at his home in Vermont, he immediately called J.C. Hall, the founder of Hallmark, and asked if there was anything that he could do to help. After giving Rockwell's offer some thought, Hall asked him to come to Kansas City and create a painting that would depict the city rebuilding itself after the flood. Rockwell eagerly agreed to do the painting suggested by Hall and he arrived in Kansas City to begin work on the project even before the flood waters had completely receded. His painting, which has become known as "The Kansas City Spirit," still hangs in Hallmark corporate headquarters.

© Hallmark Cards, Inc.

Angels We Have Heard On High

French-English

F/C C7 F Am Csus C F
o'er the plains, And the moun - tains in re - ply
C F F/C C7 F D
Ech - o - ing their joy - ous strains. Glo -
Gm C Fmaj7 B♭ C C7
- - - ri - a

F C F B♭ F/C C F D
in ex - cel - sis De - o, Glo -
Gm C Fmaj7 B♭ C C7
- - - ri - a,
F C F B♭ F/C C7 F
in ex - cel - sis De - o.
Am Csus C F
Shep - herds, why this ju - bi - lee?

C
F
F/C
C7
F
Why your joy - ous strains pro - long?
Am
Csus
C
F
What the glad - some tid - ings be
C
F
F/C
C7
F
Which in - spire your heaven - ly song?
D
Gm
C
Glo -

Fmaj7 B♭ C C7 F C F B♭
- - ri - a in ex - cel - sis
F/C C F D
De - o, Glo -
Gm C Fmaj7 B♭ C C7
- - - ri - a
F C F B♭ F/C C7 F
in ex - cel - sis De - o.

Norman
Rockwell

Away In A Manger

Music by
JAMES R. MURRAY

B♭
stars in the sky looked down where He
F
C7
F
lay, The lit - tle Lord Je - sus, a -
B♭
C7
F
sleep on the hay. The cat - tle are
B♭
F
low - ing the Ba - by a - wakes, But

C7
F
lit - tle Lord Je - sus, no cry - ing He
makes. I love thee, Lord Je - sus, look
B♭
F
C7
down from the sky, And stay by my
F
Gm7
F/A
B♭
C7
F
cra - dle till morn - ing is nigh.

Away In A Manger

Music by
JONATHAN E. SPILMAN

B♭
F
heav - ens looked down where He lay, The
chil - dren in Thy ten - der care and
F/A
F
Gm7
C7
lit - tle Lord Je - sus, a - sleep in the
take us to heav - en to live with Thee
F
C
hay. The cat - tle are low - ing, the
there. A - way in a man - ger no
G
C
poor Ba - by wakes, But lit - tle Lord
crib for His bed The lit - tle Lord

G7
Je - sus no cry - ing He
Je - sus lay down His sweet
C7
F
makes; I love Thee, Lord Je - sus, look
head. The stars in the heav - ens looked
B♭
F
F/A
down from the sky, And stay by my
down where He lay, The lit - tle Lord
F
Gm7
C7
F
cra - dle to watch lul - la - by.
Je - sus a - sleep in the hay.

Deck The Hall

Welsh

D/A A D A D A
la la la. Don we now our gay ap - par - el,
la la la. Fol - low me in mer - ry meas - ure,
la la la. Sing we joy - ous, all to - geth - er
F♯m Bm A/E E7 A D A7
Fa la la la la la la la la. Troll the an - cient
Fa la la la la la la la la. While I tell of
Fa la la la la la la la la. Heed - less of the
Bm A D G D/F♯ G D/C A7 D
Yule - tide car - ol. Fa la la la la, la la la la.
Yule - tide treas - ure. Fa la la la la, la la la la.
wind and weath - er. Fa la la la la, la la la la.

Norman Rockwell

The First Noel

French-English

Additional Lyrics

2. They looked up and saw a star
   Shining in the East, beyond them far;
   And to the earth it gave great light,
   And so it continued both day and night.

3. And by the light of that same star,
   Three wise men came from country far;
   To seek for a King was their intent,
   And to follow the star wherever it went.

4. This star drew night to the northwest,
   O'er Bethlehem it took its rest;
   And there it did both stop and stay,
   Right over the place where Jesus lay.

5. Then entered in those wise men three,
   Full reverently upon their knee;
   And offered there in His presence,
   Their gold, and myrrh, and frankincense.

Norman Rockwell

Good Christian Men, Rejoice

German, 14th Century
Words translated by JOHN M. NEALE

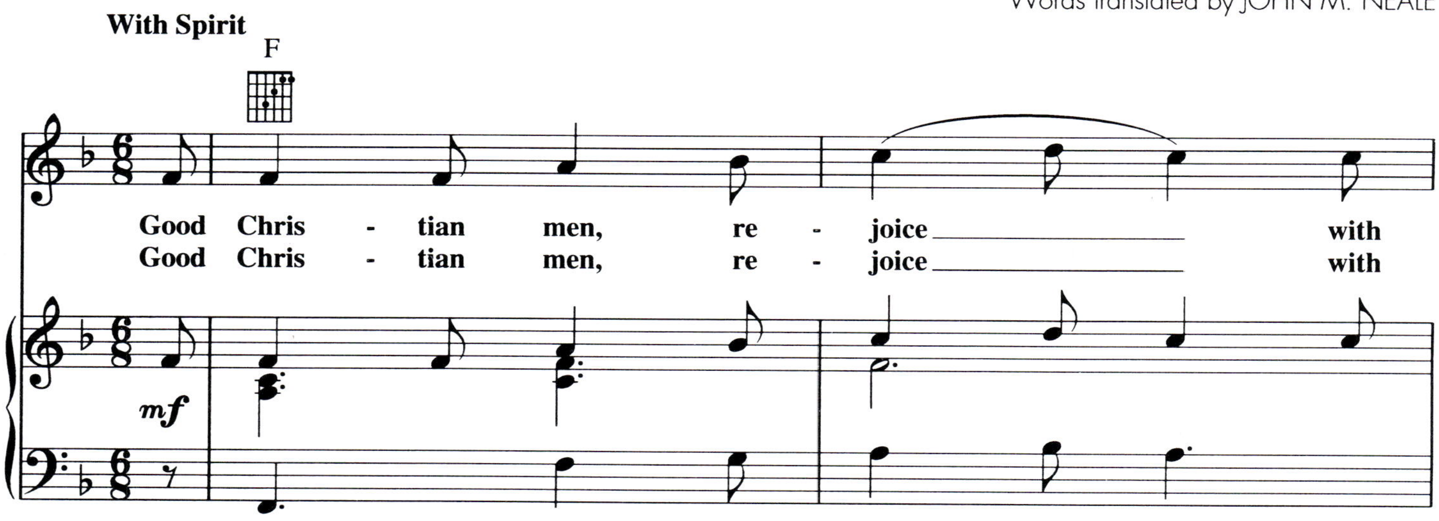
With Spirit
F
mf
Good Chris - tian men, re - joice with
Good Chris - tian men, re - joice with

heart and soul and voice,
heart and soul and voice,
B♭ F/C C♯dim Dm
Give ye heed to what we say:
Now ye hear of end - less bliss;
B♭ F/A Gm7 C7
News! News! Je - sus Christ is
Joy! Joy! Je - sus Christ was

Dm C F Bb
born to - day! Ox and ass be -
born for this. He hath ope'd the
F/C C#dim Dm Gm7 C7
fore Him bow, And He is in the
heav'n - ly door, And man is bless - ed
Dm C F Bb C7/G
man - ger now; Christ is born to -
ev - er - more. Christ was born for
F/A C F C7 F
day! Christ is born to - day!
this! Christ was born for this!

Norman
Rockwell

God Rest Ye Merry, Gentlemen

English Folk Carol,
16th Century

B♭ A Dm Gm A D Gm C F B♭ F7 B♭ F A7
born up - on this day, To save us all from Sa - tan's power when
on this bless - ed morn; To which His moth - er Ma - ry did
Dm G C F C Dm C F B♭ F
we were gone a - stray.
noth - ing take in scorn.
O tid - ings of
C7 Dm A Dm G7 C C7 Dm C7
com - fort and joy, com - fort and joy; O
F B♭ F C7 Dm A Dm
tid - ings of com - fort and joy!

© Hallmark Cards, Inc.

Hark! The Herald Angels Sing

Words by CHARLES WESLEY, 1739
Music by FELIX MENDELSSOHN, 1840

E♭
Hark! The her - ald
E♭/B♭ B♭ E♭/G Gm A♭ E♭/B♭ B♭7 E♭
an - gels sing, "Glo - ry to the new - born King!
Cm F7/A
Peace on earth, and mer - cy mild,
B♭ F7/C B♭ B♭/F F7 B♭ E♭
God and sin - ners re - con - ciled." Joy - ful all ye

B♭7/D E♭ E♭/B♭ B♭ E♭ B♭7/D E♭ B♭
na - tions rise, Join the tri - umph of the skies;
A♭ C7/G Fm C7 Fm B♭7 E♭/G
With th' an - gel - ic host pro - claim, "Christ is born in
E♭/B♭ B♭7 E♭ A♭ C7/G Fm C7 Fm
Beth - le - hem." Hark! The her - ald an - gels sing,
B♭7 E♭/G E♭/B♭ B♭7 E♭
"Glo - ry to the new - born King!"

I Heard The Bells On Christmas Day

Words by HENRY WADSWORTH LONGFELLOW
Music by JOHN BAPTISTE CALKIN

3. And in despair I bow'd my head:
"There is no peace on earth," I said,
"For hate is strong, and mocks the song
Of peace on earth, good will to men."

4. Then pealed the bells more loud and deep:
"God is not dead, nor doth He sleep;
The wrong shall fail, the right prevail,
With peace on earth, good will to men."

5. Till, ringing, singing on its way,
The world revolved from night to day,
A voice, a chime, a chant sublime,
Of peace on earth, good will to men!

Norman Rockwell

It Came Upon The Midnight Clear

Words by EDMUND H. SEARS, 1849
Music by RICHARD S. WILLIS, 1850

Bb+ Eb/Bb Bb
an - gels bend - ing near the
Eb Cm7 F7
earth, To touch their harps of
Bb
no chord
D
gold; "Peace on the
D7 Gm D Gm
earth, good will to men, From

F/C
C7
F
heav'n's all - gra - cious King."
F7
B♭
B♭+
E♭/B♭
The world in sol - emn
B♭
E♭
Cm7
still - ness lay, To hear the
F7
B♭
an - gels sing.

Norman
Rockwell

Jingle Bells

Words and Music by
J. PIERPONT

B♭
ring, Mak - ing spir - its bright, what
lank, Mis - for - tune seemed his lot, he
bay, two - for - ty for his speed, then
Gm
F/C
C7
fun it is to ride and sing a sleigh - ing song to -
got in - to a drift - ed bank and we, we got up -
hitch him to an o - pen sleigh and crack! you'll take the
F
C7
F
night! Oh!
sot! Oh!
lead! Oh!
Jin - gle bells, jin - gle bells,
F7
B♭
jin - gle all the way. Oh what fun it

F
G7
C7
is to ride in a one horse o - pen sleigh!
F
Jin - gle bells, jin - gle bells, jin - gle all the
F7
B♭
F
way. Oh what fun it is to ride in a
C7
F
one horse o - pen sleigh!
A

Norman
Rockwell

Joy To The World

ISAAC WATTS, 1719,
LOWELL MASON, 1839

With spirit
f
D
Em
D/A
A
D
Joy to the world! the Lord is come: Let
G
A7
D
earth re - ceive her King; Let ev - ery
heart pre - pare Him room, And heav-en and na - ture

A
sing, And heav-en and na-ture sing, And
D G D Em D/A A
heav-en and heav-en and na-ture
D Em D/A A
sing. He rules the world with truth and
D G A7 D
grace, And makes the na-tions prove The

glo - ries of His right - eous -
ness, And won - ders of His love, And
A D G
won - ders of His love, And won - ders,
D Em D/A A D
won - ders of His love.

O Christmas Tree

F F♯dim Gm C7
Christ - mas tree, you stand in ver - dant
Christ - mas tree, much pleas - ure doth thou
Christ - mas tree, thy can - dles shine out
Fsus F Fmaj7 D7♭9 D9
beau - ty! Your boughs are green in
bring me! For ev - 'ry year the
bright - ly! Each bough doth hold its
Gm C9 B♭dim7 F C
sum - mer's glow, and do not fade in win - ter's snow. O
Christ - mas tree brings to us all both joy and glee. O
ti - ny light that makes each toy to spark - le bright. O

F Gm/C C/B♭ A D7 Gm D Gm C7
Christ - mas tree! O Christ - mas tree, you stand in ver - dant
Christ - mas tree! O Christ - mas tree, much pleas - ure doth thou
Christ - mas tree! O Christ - mas tree, thy can - dles shine out
1,2
3
B♭dim7 F B♭dim7 F C F F/E Cm6/E♭
beau - ty! O bright - ly! O Christ - mas tree! O
bring me! O
D7sus D7 Gm D7 Gm C7 C7/F F
Christ - mas tree, thy can - dles shine out bright - ly!

© Hallmark Cards, Inc.

O Come, All Ye Faithful

JOHN FRANCIS WADE, between 1740 and 1743;
Translated by FREDERICH OAKELEY, 1852

G D
O come, all ye faithful,
Sing choirs of angels,
G D G C G/D D Em
joy - ful and tri - um - phant, O
sing in ex - ul - ta - tion, O
D A D A7 D G
come ye, O come ye to
sing all ye ci - ti - zens of
D/A A7 D G D7 G
Beth - le - hem; Come and be -
heav - en a - bove. Glo - ry to

D7sus D7 G D G Em Am
hold Him, born the King of
God in the
D G D G D7 G
an - gels; O come, let us a - dore Him, O
high - est!
D G D7 G D G D7 G D A7
come, let us a - dore Him, O come, let us a -
D D7 G C G/D D7 G
dore Him, Christ, the Lord!

O Come, O Come Emmanuel

Translated by JOHN M. NEALE
and HENRY S. COFFIN
Possibly 12th century

F C Dm
til the Son of God ap - pear. Re - joice, re -
Am F B♭ C Dm C F B♭ F/A
joice! Em - man - u - el shall come to Thee, O
Gm Dm/A Am Dm Gm
Is - ra - el! O come, Thou key of Da - vid,
Dm F B♭ Gm Dm Am Dm Gm
come And o - pen wide our heav'n - ly home. Make

Dm/A A Dm C/G G7 C Dm
safe the way that leads on high And
C Am F Gm F/C C7 F
close the path to mis - er - y. Re -
C Dm Am F B♭ C Dm C
joice, re - joice! Em - man - u - el shall
F B♭ F Gm Dm Am Dm
come to Thee, O Is - ra - el!

O Holy Night

English Words by J.S. DWIGHT
Music by ADOLPHE ADAM

F
C
C7
world in sin and er - ror pin - ing, till He ap -
break for the slave is our broth - er, and in His
Em/B
B7
Em
peared and the soul felt its worth. A
name all op - pres - sion shall cease. Sweet
G7
C
thrill of hope the wear - y world re - joic - es, for
hymns of joy in grate - ful cho - rus raise we, let
G7
C
yon - der breaks a new and glor - ious morn;
all with - in us praise His ho - ly name;

Am
Em
Fall on your knees, oh,
Christ is the Lord, oh,
Dm
Am
hear the an - gel voic - es! O
praise His name for - ev - er! His
C
G7
C/E
F
night di - vine o
pow'r and glo - ry
C
G7
C
night when Christ was born! O
ev - er - more pro - claim! His
cresc.

1
G
G7
C
F
night O ho - ly
f
C
G7
C
night O night di - vine!
2
G
G7
C/E
F
pow'r and glo - ry
cresc.
f
C
G7
C
ev - er - more pro - claim!
decresc.
p

© Hallmark Cards, Inc.

Silent Night

Words by JOSEPH MOHR
Music by FRANZ GRÜBER

Quietly
B♭
Si - lent night, ho - ly night!
Si - lent night, ho - ly night!
Si - lent night, ho - ly night!
mp

F7
B♭
All is calm, all is bright.
Shep - herds quake at the sight.
Son of God love's pure light.
E♭
B♭
Round yon Vir - gin Moth - er and Child.
Glo - ries stream from heav - en a far,
Ra - diant beams from Thy ho - ly face
E♭
B♭
Ho - ly In - fant so ten - der and
Heaven - ly hosts sing Al - le - lu -
With the dawn of re - deem - ing

F7
mild, Sleep in heav - en - ly
ia, Christ the Sav - ior is
grace, Je - sus, Lord, at Thy
mf
B♭
B♭/F
peace, Sleep in
born! Christ the
birth. Je - sus
F7
B♭
heav - en - ly peace.
Sav - ior is born!
Lord at Thy birth.

Norman Rockwell

Toyland

Words by GLEN MAC DONOUGH
Music by VICTOR HERBERT

1 E♭
C7
dwell with - in it. You are
pass its
F9
B♭7
ev - er hap - py then.
2 E♭
C7
bor - ders You can
Fm
B♭7
E♭
nev - er re - turn a - gain.

DEC.
25
24
Norman
Rockwell

The Twelve Days Of Christmas

English Folk Song,
17th or 18th Century

Repeat as needed
C7
F
B♭
F
C7
Two turtle doves,
Three French hens,
Four calling birds,
And a partridge in a pear tree.
F
D.S. for verses 3-4
On the fifth day of Christmas, my true love sent to me:
C7
F
G7
C
Five gold rings.
F
Gm
C7
Four calling birds, Three French hens, Two turtle doves, And a

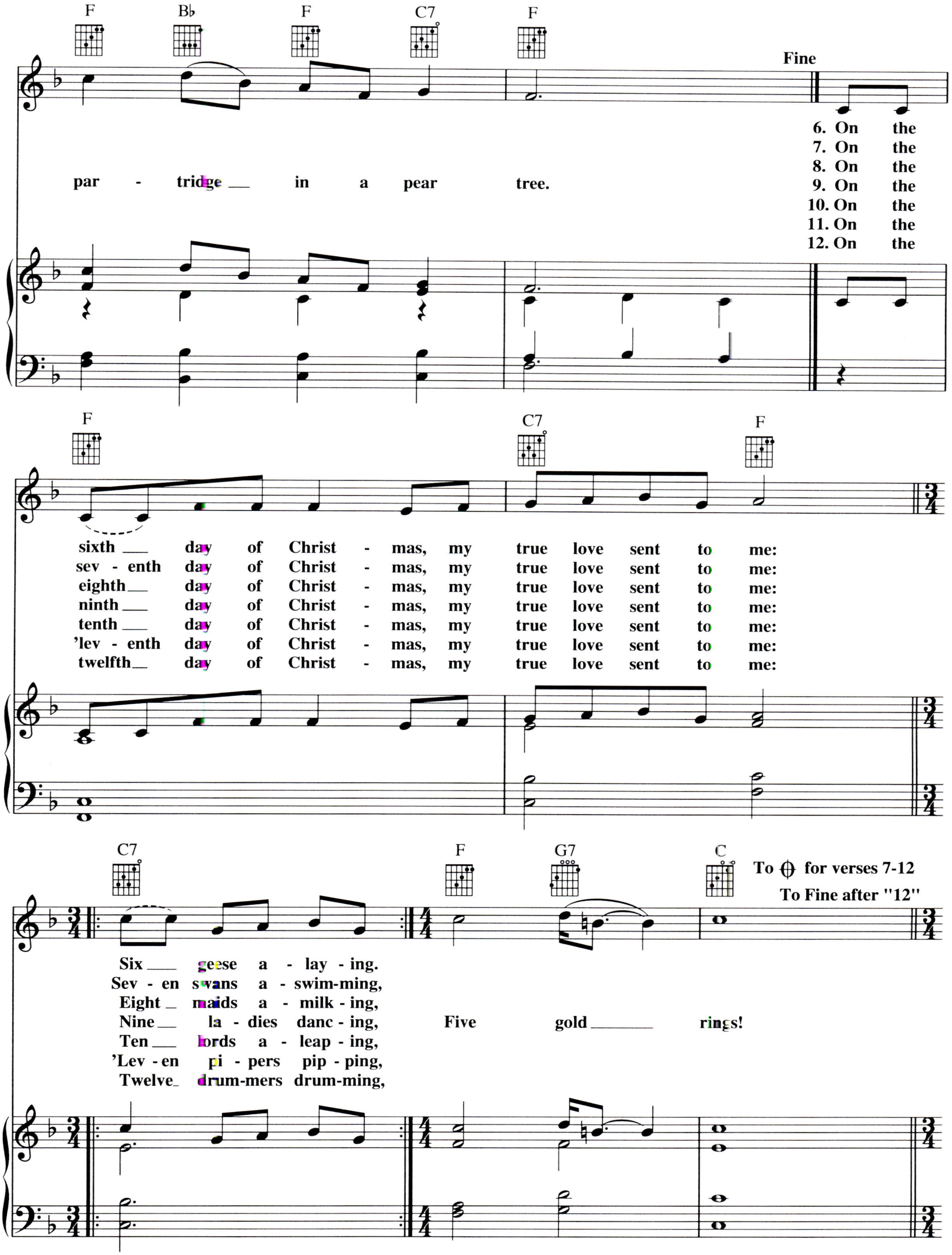
F Bb F C7 F
Fine
par - tridge __ in a pear tree.
6. On the
7. On the
8. On the
9. On the
10. On the
11. On the
12. On the
F C7 F
sixth __ day of Christ - mas, my true love sent to me:
sev - enth day of Christ - mas, my true love sent to me:
eighth __ day of Christ - mas, my true love sent to me:
ninth __ day of Christ - mas, my true love sent to me:
tenth __ day of Christ - mas, my true love sent to me:
'lev - enth day of Christ - mas, my true love sent to me:
twelfth __ day of Christ - mas, my true love sent to me:
C7 F G7 C
To ⊕ for verses 7-12
To Fine after "12"
Six __ geese a - lay - ing.
Sev - en swans a - swim-ming,
Eight _ maids a - milk - ing,
Nine __ la - dies danc - ing,
Ten __ lords a - leap - ing,
'Lev - en pi - pers pip - ping,
Twelve_ drum-mers drum-ming,
Five gold ______ rings!

Up On The Housetop

By BENJAMIN R. HANBY

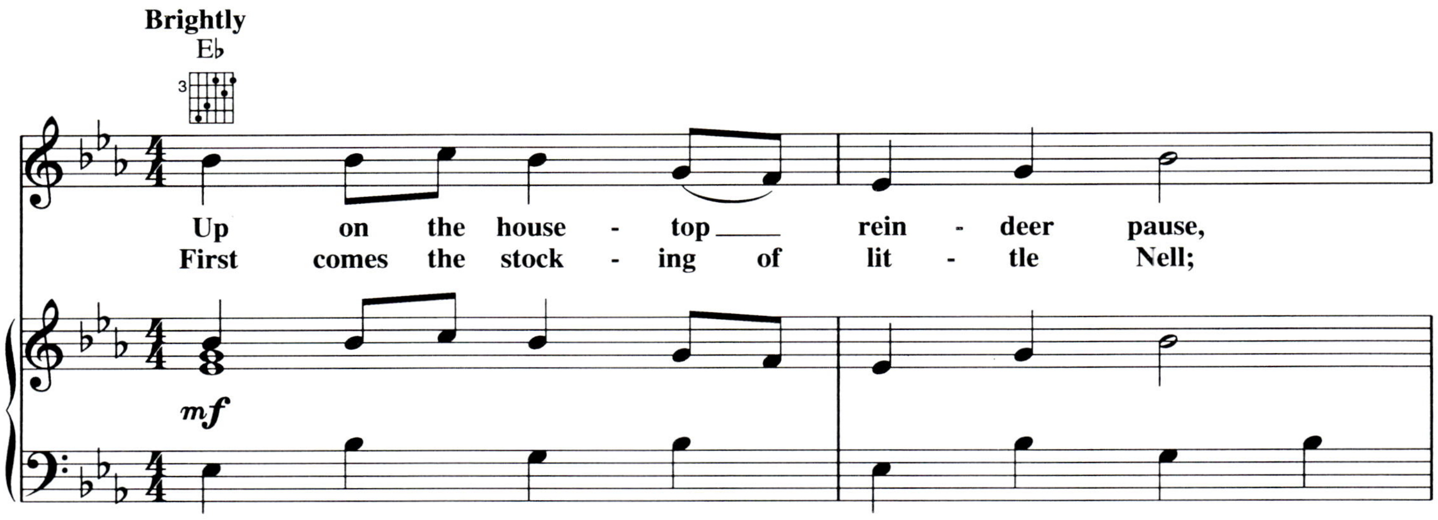
Brightly
E♭
3
mf
Up on the house - top rein - deer pause,
First comes the stock - ing of lit - tle Nell;

Ab
Eb
Bb7sus
Bb7
Out jumps good old San - ta Claus;
Oh, dear San - ta, fill it well;
Eb
Down thru the chim - ney with lots of toys,
Give her a dol - lie that laughs and cries,
Ab
Eb
Bb7sus
Bb7
Eb
All for the lit - tle ones, Christ - mas joys.
One that will o - pen and shut her eyes.
3

A♭
E♭
Ho, ho, ho, Who would - n't go!
Fm7
B♭7
E♭
Ho, ho, ho, Who would - n't go!
E♭7
A♭
E♭
A♭
Up on the house - top, click, click, click,
E♭
B♭7sus
B♭7
E♭
Down thru the chim - ney with good Saint Nick.

We Three Kings Of Orient Are

Words and Music by
JOHN H. HOPKINS, 1857

D G
Field and foun - tain, moor and moun - tain,
Am Em/B B7 Em D7
Fol - low - ing yon - der star. O
G C G
star of won - der, star of night,
C G
Star with roy - al beau - ty bright,

Em D G C G D G
West - ward lead - ing, still pro - ceed - ing,
C G
Guide us to thy per - fect light.

Norman Rockwell

O Little Town Of Bethlehem

Words by PHILLIPS BROOKS, 1868
Music by LEWIS H. REDNER, 1868

Gm F/C C7
dream - less sleep The si - lent ___ stars go
an - gels keep Their watch of ___ won - d'ring
F C7/G G♯dim A
by; Yet in thy dark streets shim - eth The
love. O morn - ing stars, to - geth - er Pro
Dm Gm A F Fdim F
ev - er - last - ing light; The hopes and fears of
claim the ho - ly birth! And prais - es sing to
F♯dim Gm Bdim F/C C7 F
all the years Are met in thee to - night.
God the King, And peace to men on earth!

Norman
Rockwell

We Wish You A Merry Christmas

English

D/B
A7
D7
G
tid - ings we bring to you and your kin, Good
D7
G
C
D7
G
tid - ings for Christ - mas and a hap - py New Year. We
C
E7
A7
D
all know that San - ta's com - ing, We all know that San - ta's com - ing, We
B7
Em
G/B
C
D7
G
all know that San - ta's com - ing, And soon will be here. Good

D/A A7 D7 G
tid - ings we bring to you and your kin, Good
D7 G C D7 G
tid - ings for Christ - mas and a hap - py New Year. We
C E7 A7 D
wish you a Mer - ry Christ - mas, We wish you a Mer - ry Christ - mas, We
B Em G/B C D7 G
wish you a Mer - ry Christ - mas, and a hap - py New Year.

Norman
Rockwell

What Child Is This?

English

D
greet with an - thems sweet While
kings sal - va - tion brings, Let
C
B7
Em
shep - herds watch are keep -
lov - ing hearts en - throne
Bm
G
ing? This, this is
Him. Raise, raise the
D
Bm
Em
Christ the King, Whom shep - herds
song on high, The Vir - gin

C
B7
guard and an - gels sing:
sings her lul - la - by:
G
F#m
Haste, haste to bring him
Joy, joy for Christ is
Bm
Em
laud, The babe, the
born, The babe, the
B7
Em
son of Ma - ry.
son of Ma - ry.

Norman Rockwell